MICHIGAN

A PHOTOGRAPHIC CELEBRATION

compiled by the staff of
American & World Geographic Publishing

Above: *Rushing to Lake Superior: Gorge Falls on the Black River in western Upper Peninsula.*

Title page: *Over one of Michigan's freshwater ponds a birch bends to admire its fall colors.* STAN OSOLINSKI

Front cover: *One of Michigan's brightest-colored treasures: autumn in the Upper Peninsula's Porcupine Mountains State Park.* TOM TILL

Back cover, top: *Renaissance Center, Detroit.* STAN OSOLINSKI
Bottom right: *Autumn farmscape near Gilead.* GEORGE WUERTHNER
Left: *Canada geese enjoying a spring swim.* STAN OSOLINSKI

Above: Lake Superior sunrise over Pt. Isabella; Keweenaw Peninsula.
Right: Who will find the biggest huckleberry in Luce County?

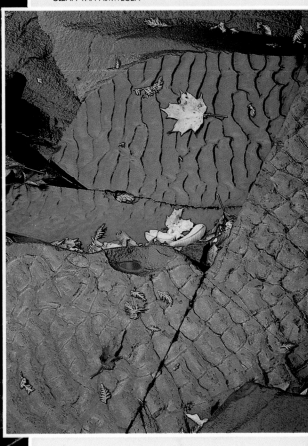

5

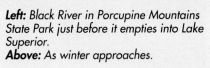

Left: *Black River in Porcupine Mountains State Park just before it empties into Lake Superior.*
Above: *As winter approaches.*

JIM CRONK

ROBERT MAUST

6

Michigan agriculture:
Above: Corn harvest, Western Michigan.
Left top: Celery planting, Bryon Center.
Left bottom: A Huron County farm.

Above: Winter reflections in Ottawa County.

Facing page: A stream still manages to make its way even as winter tries to stop it.

STAN OSOLINSKI

JIM CRONK

Left: Winter nestles in as fall tries to hold on.
Above: "I think I had a nibble." Ice fishing in Hamilton.

JIM CRONK

Above right: Michigan is proud of its many ethnic communities, including Holland where the Dutch settled.

Facing page, top: Winter on the farm, Western Michigan.
Bottom: One of a handful of covered bridges in the Grand Rapids area.

Above left: *Munising Falls in Pictured Rocks National Lakeshore, Upper Peninsula.*
Above right: *An unusual, calm autumn day on Lake Superior.*
Facing page: *Coho fishermen at sunset in Ludington State Park.*

16

Left: Warming the hands while the scenery warms the soul along Hemingway's beloved Little Two Hearted River.
Above: Time-honored traditions complement autumn; Amish farmers.

Facing page: Peaceful waters found near Detroit's urban center: Kensington Metropolitan Park.

STAN OSOLINSKI

STAN OSOLINSKI

Left: *A Great Lake's autumn shoreline.*
Above: *Red squirrel banqueting in Kensington Metropolitan Park.*

Above: *Finally! Away from traffic.*

Facing page: *One of Michigan's friendly characters, a raccoon.*

Left: *"Going up, please." The Soo Locks at Sault Ste. Marie raise ships from all over the world to Lake Superior's level.*
Above: *At the top of Michigan's Lower Peninsula, Fort Michilimackinac looks out on the link between Michigan's peninsulas—Mackinac Bridge.*

Facing page: *Largest of the Great Lakes: Lake Superior.*

Above: Winding through Southeastern Michigan, the Huron River provides recreational opportunities to Detroit-area residents.
Right: In the stillness of the morning on one of Michigan's many inland lakes.

Above: A pair of northern bald eagles discuss breakfast possibilities; Seney National Wildlife Refuge, Upper Peninsula.
Facing page: Quietly and peacefully flowing toward Lake Erie; William Holliday Park west of Detroit.

Left: Color returns to the forest; bloodroot blossom.
Above: Spanning the Flat River.

Facing page: Munising Falls as it attempts to carry logs to Lake Superior.

RICHARD LONGSETH

JIM CRONK

Left: One of Michigan's favorite vacation sites, Great Bear Dunes and Lake Michigan.
Above: One honker in, one honker out, along Lake Superior.

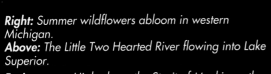

Right: Summer wildflowers abloom in western Michigan.
Above: The Little Two Hearted River flowing into Lake Superior.

Facing page: High above the Strait of Mackinac, the Natural Arch is one of the wonderful sights on Mackinac Island.

35

Left: *Just west of St. Ignace on U.S. 2, the Cut River Bridge provides a spectacular view of morning fog lifting out of the forest.*
Above: *The pace is leisurely on Mackinac Island, where motorized vehicles are banned.*

Above: *Lake Superior surf after a storm, Keweenaw Peninsula.*

Facing page: *The winter surf on Lake Michigan can get pretty rough.*

JIM CRONK

39

Above: *"Let's hope the wind doesn't come up," in Holland.*
Left: *Autumn maples near Gilead.*

JIM CRONK

GLENN VAN NIMWEGEN

Right: *Some work hard to get where they are going and some go wherever the wind takes them; at the Mackinac Bridge.*
Above: *God's artwork: Lake of the Clouds in the Porcupine Mountains.*

Facing page: *Michigan's forests have many colors to display every autumn.*

ULRICH TUTSCH

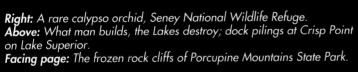

Right: *A rare calypso orchid, Seney National Wildlife Refuge.*
Above: *What man builds, the Lakes destroy; dock pilings at Crisp Point on Lake Superior.*
Facing page: *The frozen rock cliffs of Porcupine Mountains State Park.*

44

STAN OSOLINSKI

45

Left: *The last traces of sunlight reflect on Greenwood Lake.*
Above: *Pines keeping each other company during the long winter.*

JIM CRONK PHOTOS ABOVE AND BELOW

Above: Autumn's colors approach the Upper Peninsula's Sturgeon River.

Facing page, top: "Are they biting, son?" Perch fishing in Luce County.

Bottom: Canoeing down the Boardman River near Traverse City.

Left: Thirteen-lined ground squirrel.
Above: Winter's gone and the trees are budding on the Upper Peninsula.

Facing page. The tallest waterfall in Michigan: Laughing Whitefish Falls, Upper Peninsula.

Kensington Metroplitan Park:
Left: *The sun is trying to work its way through fog on Kent Lake.*
Above: *Geese swimming in liquid gold.*

53

Right: Located in the heart of Lansing near the Grand River is Michigan's capitol. Lansing is probably better known as the home of Ervin "Magic" Johnson.
Above: Night in Detroit as it appears from Belle Isle in the Detroit River.

Facing page: A Great Lakes winter sunset.

Left: *Ready for harvest; a wheat field in Shiawassee County.*
Above: *Swamp patterns of grasses and snow as spring approaches; Kensington Metropolitan Park.*

Scenes at Holland:
Right: Sailing into the safe harbor at Lake Macatawa.
Above: Providing a guiding light to those lost in a storm: Holland Harbor Lighthouse.

Facing page: De Zwann, Windmill Island, is a sign of Dutch immigrants who settled in Western Michigan.

Above: *"The perfect pumpkin is in here somewhere, probably in this crate…" Farm market, Western Michigan.*
Right: *Basking in the sunlight with memories of more productive years.*

Left: *Resting for the winter in the Upper Peninsula.*
Above: *Growing up together.*

Left: Spring, one hopes, is just around the corner.
Above: The Upper Peninsula's Tahquamenon Falls, second-largest in the United States east of the Mississippi.

Facing page: Ice columns formed by the mist from Tahquamenon Falls.

Above: *Waiting for the youngsters: a killdeer.*
Facing page: *Guiding ships on Lake Superior, Crisp Point Lighthouse.*

GLENN VAN NIMWEGEN PHOTOS BOTH PAGES

Left: Autumn's red sumac watches the Presque Isle River flow.
Above: Sometimes a seed will sprout no matter where it falls; Lake Superior shoreline, Porcupine Mountains.

STAN OSOLINSKI

Above: Sunrise at Isle Royale National Park in Lake Superior.
Right: Looking down at Lake of the Clouds, Porcupine Mountains State Park.

GLENN VAN NIMWEGEN

Right: From blue to white: That's what happens as water descends Tahquamenon Falls.
Above: Summer's in full swing at Seney National Wildlife Refuge.

Facing page: The river has a thousand different ways to fall; Bond Falls, Upper Peninsula.

STAN OSOLINSKI

Above: *Mackinac Island and its ferries.*
Right: *The rocky Lake Superior shore.*

73

Above: *Ice building up on frozen Lake Michigan.*
Right: *Pea-soup fog on the ground, but the skies are clear.*

Above: Frozen Munising Falls at Pictured Rocks National Lakeside.

Facing page: Snow and ice pushed up along Lake Superior's shore.

Above: As bright a yellow as the sun they reach for:
wildflowers in Western Michigan.
Right: The Gerald Ford Museum in Michigan's second-
largest city, Grand Rapids.

Above: *Truly one of the engineering marvels of the world, the brightly lit Mackinac Bridge stretches between Michigan's peninsulas.*

Facing page: *The Sturgeon River cuts through the Upper Peninsula landscape.*

Above: *Cutting hay on a beautiful Western Michigan farm.*
Top left: *A moose takes refreshment.*
Left: *Farm-fresh produce at Detroit's Eastern Market.*

Above: Hart Plaza Fountain on the Detroit River in downtown Detroit.
Left: A glassblower demonstrates his skill at Greenfield Village, Dearborn.

Above: Sunset at Pictured Rocks National Shoreline.

Facing page: The spring runoff has made this traveler glad that he brought his canoe along.

STAN OSOLINSKI

SHARON CUMMINGS/M.L. DEMBINSKY, JR. PHOTOGRAPHY ASSOC.

Above: Sunrise in the forest.
Right: At the Michigan Speedway.

Facing page: Sweeping away the leaves at Munising Falls.

Above: Skiers enjoy a lift at Bittersweet Mountain, Otsego.
Right: Mackinac Island, where world-famous fudge is served.

Above: Lake Huron is held back by the breakwater at Port Austin.

Facing page: The Ambassador Bridge spans the Detroit River and connects Detroit with Windsor, Ontario.

Overleaf: The sun sets on Kensington Metropolitan Park.